SMUDGE, THE LITTLE LOST LAMB

James Herriot

Illustrated by Ruth Brown

St. Martin's Press
New York

Copyright © 1991 by James Herriot   Illustrations copyright © 1991 by Ruth Brown   Printed in the U.S.A.   ISBN 0-312-11067-7 LC 91-19201

Harry had got up very early in the morning to help his father with the lambs. He had enjoyed holding the ewe and then rubbing down the newborn lambs with straw to dry them. He liked all the animals on the farm, and often helped his father with the cows, calves and pigs, but spring was his favorite time, when the lambs were born.

'They are grand, strong lambs,' said Farmer Cobb, looking down at the twin lambs who were standing in the pen by their mother. 'It was very good of you to get up early to help me, Harry. Would you like to have these two lambs for yourself?'

'Oh, yes please, Dad,' said Harry.

'All right then, they're yours. You must keep an eye on them every day. What are you going to call them?'

Harry thought for a moment. 'That one has got a funny white mark on his nose. I'll call him Smudge - and his sister can be Smartie.'

'Those are good names. Now it's time you got ready for school, so off you go.'

A few days later, Harry was with his father when all the ewes and lambs were turned out into the field. Farmer Cobb looked at the flock spreading out across the wide expanse of grass. There were about a hundred ewes, most of them with twin lambs but some with just one and a few with three. The field had walls on three sides, but where it met the lane there were posts and wire.

'I hope I've fastened that wire down tightly enough,' he said.

'Some of these Swaledale lambs will try to get underneath it. In fact, some aren't happy until they've found a way out of the field.'

Farmer Cobb didn't know it at the time, but Smudge was one of those lambs.

For three weeks the flock grazed in the spring sunshine, the ewes cropping the young grass and the lambs playing happily and enjoying their mothers' milk. One of the lambs' favorite games was to collect in little groups and dash up and down by the side of a wall. Harry used to laugh when he saw them racing along, leaping joyfully in the air.

However, among the happy throng there was one lamb who wasn't content and that was Smudge. He enjoyed the games well enough, but every day he had a growing urge to see what was outside the field. He was getting very tired of seeing only the walls and the stretch of wire. In fact, at the age of three weeks, Smudge was bored.

He longed to escape and see what the world was like outside, and surely, he thought, there was some way he could get under that wire. Each day he worked his way along, nosing at where the wire met the grass, but Farmer Cobb had done his job well. Smudge was about to give up hope when, one morning, he found a tiny gap. He was able to get his nose through; then, as he thrust and pushed, he got his neck, then all his body, through and with a final wriggle he found himself on the other side.

Oh, the sensation of freedom was wonderful as he looked up and down the pretty little country road. He could go wherever he pleased, the whole world was his to explore, and he felt quite sorry for all his friends still imprisoned in the field. Oh, how clever he had been, he thought, as he puffed out his little chest and strutted along to the bend in the lane.

He could see for miles down a long valley. There were cattle and Dales ponies grazing on the green slopes which ran down to a pebbly river spanned by a fine stone bridge with three arches.

He gazed wonderingly at this new sight for some time; then he nibbled at the long grass by the road before running and skipping gleefully in the other direction. He was thrilled to be able to see the battlements of a ruined castle towering over the roofs of the village a mile away.

This was such fun! He leaped high in the air for sheer joy. He felt so important: none of the other lambs knew anything of this fascinating world outside the field. As he trotted around, picking at the grass, looking eagerly around him, he knew that this was what he had always wanted.

However, after about an hour of exploration, Smudge glanced through the wire and could see his sister Smartie suckling her mother, her tail wagging furiously. Suddenly he realised that he was hungry. He decided he would slip back and have some of that lovely milk before coming out again later. After all, he could do just as he liked now.

He pushed his nose at the wire. But where was the gap? It wasn't where he thought it should be. As he worked his way along without finding an opening, his heart beat faster, and when he tried again and again without success he began to feel really frightened and baa'd loudly for his mother. She replied to his shrill call with a deep baa but she couldn't do anything to help. Soon there was a deafening chorus of Smudge's high-pitched baa and his mother's deep one.

All he wanted now was to get back into the field, but his fear turned to terror as a huge dog came along the lane and rushed at him, barking and snarling.

Smudge ran away as fast as he could, and just as the dog was about to catch him, he dived between the bars of a gate into a field on the other side of the lane.

He was safe from the dog who couldn't get through, but Smudge found himself looking up into the face of an enormous bull. He had never seen such a monster and when the bull bent down until the shining bronze ring in his nose almost touched the lamb's face, Smudge fled at even greater speed.

He ran and ran and ran over the pasture until he came to a gate which opened on to the main road. He looked back. The bull was still lumbering after him, probably just out of curiosity, but Smudge, in his panic, shot straight across the road between the speeding cars and a bus whose startled passengers stared out at him.

He soon found himself on the outskirts of a village where he hid in a shed. He stayed there for ages, too frightened to move, but when it was dark he ventured out into a strange, unfamiliar world. Where was he? Where was his field with his mother and Smartie; how he longed for them. As he walked slowly along the road he felt hungrier than ever and was now exceedingly tired. He was so weak he could hardly do more than stagger from side to side.

Then, in the darkness, a bitter wind sprang up, blowing little flakes of snow into his face. Within a few minutes the kind of blizzard which sometimes appears without warning in the Yorkshire spring was raging around him.

S mudge's faltering steps took him to a cottage, just visible
in the darkness, and he huddled against the gate. He
tried to find some protection from the driving snow, but
there was no shelter and he did not have the strength to
walk any further. He felt very, very tired and very, very cold
and as he curled himself up and fell asleep, the big flakes of
snow fell steadily on his body.

Penny Robinson was returning from her music lesson with
her mother and was about to go through the gate when she
noticed the little heap of snow at her feet. She pushed at it
with her shoe, and, as she cleared the snow away with her
hand, she cried out in surprise.

'Oh, look, Mummy! There's a tiny dead lamb under the
snow!'

'A lamb? It can't be!' exclaimed Mrs Robinson.

Penny looked closer. 'It is, it is, and maybe he's not dead. I
think he's still breathing.'

S he picked Smudge up in her arms and hurried down the garden path. Inside the house she put him on the kitchen table where he lay very still with his eyes closed.

Penny brushed the snow from him and rubbed him with a towel, but he did not move and his wool stayed damp and bedraggled.

'We must get him warm or he'll die,' said Penny. Then she had an idea. She ran up to the bedroom and fetched her mother's hairdryer and began to blow warm air on to the tiny body. Again and again she sent the heat from the dryer from head to tail and back again, waiting for some signs of life from the little creature.

From way down in the depths of his icy sleep, Smudge became aware of the delicious warmth swirling around him like a summer breeze, thawing him out, drying his wool, pulling him back into the world. It was like a lovely dream - as though he was back with his mother on the sunny hillside field. When he opened his eyes and looked up into Penny's face, she laughed in delight.

'Look, look, it's working! He's coming around!' She continued using the dryer, fluffing up the wool until it looked just the same as when Smudge had left the field. But still the little lamb didn't move.

He's so weak, he needs some food,' Penny said. 'Where is the bottle I had when I was a baby?'

Mrs Robinson laughed and got the bottle from a cupboard, filled it with warm milk and gave it to Penny.

When Smudge felt the teat in his mouth he knew what to do. He had hardly any strength left, but he could still suck and the level in the bottle went down rapidly. Penny refilled the bottle and Smudge sucked again until his little stomach was full to bursting.

He began to feel much better and he looked around him at yet another strange place, the cosy kitchen with its cheerful fire. It was all new to him, but much better than the cold world outside.

Penny made a bed for him in a cardboard box by the fireside and he drifted into a deep contented sleep.

Next morning Penny was delighted to find him out of the box, and running round the room.

'What shall I do with him?' she asked her mother. 'He's so sweet – can I keep him as a pet?'

'I don't think that would be very convenient,' replied her mother. 'He's going to grow up into a big sheep and we only have a small garden. We must try to find out something about him.'

Penny gave him another bottle of milk and then went off to the school in the village.

When the teacher came in Penny put up her hand and told the class about the lamb she had found.

'Well, that is interesting,' said the teacher. 'I wonder where he came from.'

As she spoke, Harry Cobb, who was in Penny's class, put up his hand and jumped to his feet. 'Please, Miss, we lost a lamb yesterday. He was really my lamb, my father gave him to me, and he was missing when I got home from school.' He turned towards the girl and held out his hands. 'Is he about this size, Penny? And does he have a black face with a white mark on his nose?'

'Yes,' she replied.

'Well, that's Smudge! That's my lamb!'

After school that day, the snow had melted away and
Farmer Cobb went down to the village in his car to
collect Smudge. Penny went back to the farm with them,
and she and Harry watched as the little lamb was reunited
with his mother and sister in the sunny field.

They laughed as Smudge and Smartie pushed their heads
under the ewe and sucked happily, their little tails twirling.

'He's all right now, Penny, thanks to you,' Harry said. 'You
saved his life.'

Penny laughed. 'It was really the hairdryer that saved him.'

There was only one thought in Smudge's mind as he
enjoyed his mother's milk. This was where he wanted to be.
He would never ever try to get out of the field again.